British Birds

Clare Collinson

W

FRANKLIN WATTS

LONDON•SYDNEY

First published in 2015 by
Franklin Watts
338 Euston Road
London NW1 3BH

Franklin Watts Australia
Level 17/207 Kent Street
Sydney NSW 2000

HB ISBN: 978 1 4451 3635 6
Library ebook ISBN: 978 1 4451 3637 0

Dewey classification number: 598.1

Planning and production by Discovery Books Limited
Managing Editor: Laura Durman
Editor: Clare Collinson
Design: sprout.uk.com
Picture research: Clare Collinson

Printed in China

Franklin Watts is a division of Hachette Children's Books, an Hachette UK Company.
www.hachette.co.uk

Photo acknowledgements: Alamy: p. 7t (Photoshot Holdings Ltd), p. 9l (Anna Bartosch-Carlile), p. 13b (blickwinkel), p. 15t (William Leaman), p. 23t (Oliver Smart); Bigstock: p. 29t (Gilbertdestoke); FLPA: p. 5 (Malcolm Schuyl), p. 8b (Roger Wilmshurst), p. 10 (ImageBroker/Imagebroker), p. 12 (Marcel van Kammen/Minden Pictures), p. 17t (Mike Jones), p. 25t (Martin B Withers), p. 25b (Donald M. Jones/Minden Pictures); Shutterstock: title page (jeeaa. CHC), pp. 3, 31 (YK, Eric Isselee, taviphoto), p. 4 (Kletr), p. 6 (Allegresse Photography), p. 7b (red-feniks), p. 8t (Sue Robinson), p. 9r (Richard Winston), p. 11t (Vitaly Ilyasov), p. 11b (Martin Pateman), pp. 13t, 17b (Erni), p. 14 (Gallinago_media), p. 15b (maggee), p. 16 (TCreativeMedia), p. 18 (Denis Omelchenko), p. 19t (mitzy), p. 19b (TheModernCanvas), p. 20l (EBFoto), p. 20r (Martin Fowler), p. 21t (S.Cooper Digital), p. 21b (Vetapi), p. 22l (Menno Schaefer), p. 22r (Targn Pleiades), p. 23b (Vladimir Kogan Michael), p. 24 (Stanislav Duben), p. 26t (Glenn Young), p. 26b (MVPhoto), p. 27t (aleksandr hunta), p. 27b (Panu Ruangjan), p. 28t (Stephen Rees), p. 28b (David Fowler), p. 29b (V. Belov), p. 30l (Dr. Morley Read), p. 30r (ultimathule), p. 31 (Aksenova Natalya, Marina Jay, S-F, Robert Eastman, Adam Gryko, cmnaumann).

Cover photo: Shutterstock (Victor Tyakht).

Useful websites

British Trust for Ornithology
www.bto.org
Information about Britain's birds, what they do and where they live. There are videos to help with identification, as well as information about the population of different species and surveys you can take part in.

RSPB
www.rspb.org.uk
The website of the Royal Society for the Protection of Birds, with descriptions of all British birds by name and family, help with identification, as well as audio clips of bird songs and calls. There is information about the RSPB's 200 nature reserves, and you can find out about wildlife events taking place near you.

The Wildlife Trusts UK
www.wildlifetrusts.org
Discover more about British birds and other wildlife. There is a species explorer page that will help with identification. You can also find out about good places to see birds of prey and large flocks of wading birds in the UK.

Wild About Britain
www.wildaboutbritain.co.uk
Encyclopedic information about British wildlife.

Wildlife Watch: Birds
www.wildlifewatch.org.uk/explore-wildlife/animals/birds
Find out how to take part in a 'wildlife watch' and other events in your local area. You can create your own 'spotting sheets' from the A–Z of British birds.

Woodland Trust Nature Detectives: Bird pack
www.naturedetectives.org.uk/packs/birds.htm
Lots of bird activities to download and print.

Every effort has been made to ensure that these websites contain no inappropriate or offensive material. However, because of the nature of the Internet, it is impossible to guarantee that the contents of these sites will not be altered. We strongly advise that Internet access is supervised by a responsible adult.

Contents

Words that appear in **bold** in the text are explained in the glossary.

Your neighbourhood

No matter where you live in Britain, you will find a huge variety of bird life in your neighbourhood. From colourful blue tits to powerful peregrines, all birds are fascinating to watch.

Your local patch

The great thing about birds is that you don't have to go far to spot them! You probably already know the names of many of the birds you see regularly, such as sparrows and robins. The more you discover about the birds in your local area, the more interesting they become.

Other habitats to explore

All birds have a favourite place to live, called a **habitat**. You will find many of Britain's best-loved birds in gardens and parks. But once you start exploring woodlands, hedgerows, fields and coasts, you will be amazed how many different kinds you find.

Seasonal highlights

Birds are interesting to watch throughout the year, but there are some seasonal highlights to enjoy. In spring, listen for blackbirds singing from the rooftops. In summer, look out for swifts and swallows in the sky. In autumn, **wading birds** gather on seashores, and in winter you can see huge flocks of starlings swirling through the sky.

You will see blue tits in gardens, woodlands and hedgerows all over Britain. You can recognise one by its bright blue cap and the black line through its eye.

Identifying birds

You don't have to be an expert to enjoy watching birds. But if you see a bird you don't recognise, it's natural to wonder what kind it is. This book will help you **identify** many of the birds you might see around you. It also tells you something about what they do, where they live and what kinds of sounds they make.

*Peregrines are large **predators** that feed on other birds, such as pigeons. You can see them hunting on rocky coasts and even in some British cities.*

What is a bird?

Birds are a group of animals that have certain things in common.
- **They are all covered in feathers.**
- **They have two wings, although not all birds can fly.**
- **All birds have beaks, or bills.**
- **They all lay eggs.**
- **Their legs and feet are covered in small scales.**

Sparrows and starlings

One of the best ways to get to know the birds in your neighbourhood is to start close to your home. You may only have to look out of your window to see sparrows and starlings.

Chirpy sparrows

House sparrows often use our homes for their nest sites and feed in our gardens and parks. You will know you have them as neighbours if you hear lots of noisy chirping and cheeping!

Bibs and stripes

One way to identify a bird is to look at the colour and pattern of its feathers, or its plumage. A male house sparrow (below right) has a brown back, streaked with black, a grey cap and a black bib. The female (below left) has a pale band behind her eye and no black bib.

In decline

The number of house sparrows and starlings in Britain has declined greatly in recent years. You can find out about the possible reasons for this on the website of the British Trust for Ornithology (see page 2).

Sparrows often visit bird baths in the summer. Bathing in water keeps their feathers in good condition and helps them to keep cool.

Starlings gather together in huge swirling flocks called murmurations.

Pointy beaks

The shape of a bird's beak is often a clue to the kind of food it eats. A starling's beak is long, pointed and sharp – perfect for plucking insect **grubs** from the ground.

Rattles and whistles

If you hear some gurgles, rattles and whistles coming from a rooftop, look up and you'll probably see some starlings. Starlings are known for their varied songs. They also have a gift for imitating just about anything, from other birds to telephones!

Starling spectacle

In autumn and winter, vast numbers of starlings gather together to rest, or roost. Before settling down for the night, they perform one of nature's most impressive displays. Many thousands of starlings move together, creating spectacular patterns in the sky.

In autumn and winter, a starling has white speckles. If you see one close up, notice how its feathers shine with purple and green.

Garden songbirds

In springtime, gardens, parks and woodlands throughout Britain come alive with the sound of birdsong. Among the greatest singers of all are blackbirds, robins and song thrushes. Even the tiny wren can make itself heard!

Star singer

The blackbird has one of the most musical voices of all British birds. Its song sounds a little like a flute. With its jet-black feathers and orange-yellow beak, the male is easy to recognise. Females have brown feathers, often with streaks on their chests.

Songs and calls

During the **breeding season** in spring and early summer, many male birds sing to attract females, and to tell other birds to keep away from their **territory**. Birds also have calls, which you can hear all year round. They use these to communicate with each other.

In spring and early summer, listen for blackbirds singing from the rooftops and from high up in trees.

Snail smasher

Song thrushes have declined in numbers in recent years, but you can still hear them singing their tuneful songs in parks, gardens and woodlands. They feed on worms, berries, insects and snails.

Song thrushes break into snails by smashing their shells against hard ground.

The robin is one of the few birds that sings almost all year round, even in the winter.

Listening to birdsong

Knowing a bird by its song or call is a good way to identify it from a distance. You can listen to the sounds different birds make on the RSPB website (see page 2).

Robin red breast
With its little red breast and cheeky attitude, the robin is probably Britain's best-loved bird. These friendly little songbirds are a familiar sight in parks and gardens all through the year.

It's my home!
Robins may look cute, but they can be aggressive towards other birds. They are fierce defenders of their territory, and sing loudly to keep other robins away.

Wrens are the most common breeding birds in Britain. They can live almost anywhere, from gardens to remote mountains.

Tiny but loud
At only 9–10 cm long, the wren is one of the smallest birds in Britain, but it has a surprisingly loud singing voice. Its song is a series of warbles and high-pitched trills, and its **alarm call** is a loud 'teck, teck, teck'.

Finches

One of the best ways to recognise a member of the finch family is by the shape of its beak. All finches have strong, triangular beaks that are perfect for eating seeds.

Colourful chaffinches

If there's a chaffinch in your neighbourhood, you will hear its 'pink, pink' call all day long in spring. With his rusty-pink breast and cheeks, white wing patches and bluish cap, the male is strikingly colourful. The female is a paler, yellowish brown.

Neat nests

Chaffinches build neat bowl-shaped nests in trees and bushes, often finding a fork in the branches to make the nest secure. Their nests are made from moss, with a cosy lining of feathers, hair and wool.

Bringing up the brood

The female chaffinch lays between four and five eggs. When the chicks hatch, the parents feed them on insects and caterpillars. After about two weeks, the chicks will be ready to leave the nest.

Like many birds, chaffinches live in the warmth and shelter of their nest for the first few weeks of their lives. They cannot find food for themselves until after they have left the nest.

You will know a male bullfinch by its bright pinkish-red breast and cheeks and its neat black cap. The female is more drab, with a pinkish-grey chest.

Perching birds

Finches belong to a group of birds called passerines, or perching birds. Passerines have three toes pointing forwards and one pointing backwards, which enables them to perch on branches and wires. More than half of all bird species belong to this group.

Shy bullfinches

You won't often see bullfinches in gardens, as they mostly live in woodlands. They love to feed on seeds and berries. In spring, when berries are hard to find, they will feast on the buds of fruit trees.

Exotic goldfinches

With its bright red face and yellow wing patch, a goldfinch looks rather exotic. Goldfinches are more common in Britain than ever before, and you will often see them in gardens and parks. Listen for their jaunty, twittering song and call.

*In winter, look out for goldfinches feeding on seeds from thistles and spiny **teasel** heads.*

The tit family

If you see some colourful birds flitting around your neighbourhood in groups, they're likely to be members of the tit family. You can see these active little birds searching for food in gardens, parks and woodlands.

Great tits

Great tits are the largest members of the tit family. You'll know one by its black head and the black stripe running down its yellow front.

Tea-cher, tea-cher

Great tits sometimes sound a little like squeaky bicycle pumps. They make a variety of noises, but their 'tea-cher, tea-cher' call is one of the easiest birdsongs to recognise.

Great tits are among the most frequent visitors to bird feeders, especially in winter, when insects can be hard to find.

Feeding time

A good way to attract birds is to provide them with extra food. Put a bird feeder where you can see it easily, and keep it well stocked throughout the year. You will be amazed at how many birds will visit.

Long-tailed tits

With their long tails, tiny bodies and fluffy, pink-tinged plumage, long-tailed tits are among the cutest members of the tit family. They are expert nest-builders, taking up to three weeks to construct their purse-shaped nests. They use **moss**, **lichen** and feathers, and weave the nest together with **spider silk**. This acts a bit like elastic, so the nest can expand as the chicks grow.

Long-tailed tits collect as many as 2,000 feathers for their cosy nests.

Setting up home

Blue tits like to make their nests in holes in trees, but they also use nest boxes nailed to trees or walls. The female builds a cup-shaped nest from moss and dried grass, and lines it with soft feathers. When the home is ready, she lays between seven and thirteen eggs.

Growing chicks

After their eggs have hatched, blue tits feed their growing young on caterpillars. This is a busy time for both parents.

Blue tits need to find about a hundred caterpillars a day for each one of their hungry chicks!

13

Swifts, swallows and house martins

In summer, look up in the air and around the rooftops and you might see swifts, swallows or house martins twisting and turning in the sky.

Summer visitors

Swifts, swallows and house martins are long-distance **migrators**. They arrive in Britain from Africa in the spring to breed and raise their young. In the autumn, they gather together in flocks before flying thousands of kilometres back to Africa for the winter.

Soaring swifts

On bright summer days, look out for swifts soaring gracefully high up in the sky. You might get closer views in the evening, when groups of swifts fly fast and low, catching insects near to the ground. Listen for their loud screaming calls.

A life in the air

Except when they are nesting, swifts spend all their time in the air. They feed, drink, mate and even sleep **on the wing.** They have tiny feet, with four toes that usually all point forwards. They can cling to upright surfaces, but they can hardly walk and, unlike passerines, they cannot perch on branches or wires.

Swifts can reach speeds of over 110 kph!

Swallows have red chins and forked tails with long 'streamers'.

Permanent homes

If you see a bird's nest made of mud, do not disturb it, even in the autumn when the nest is empty. Swallows, swifts and house martins often return to the same nest every year.

Nesting swallows

Look out for nesting swallows in outhouses and barns. Swallows build cup-shaped nests from mud and straw. If you are lucky, you might see some baby swallows poking their heads out of the nest.

House martins

House martins also make nests of mud, but they like to build them in the **eaves** of houses in villages and towns. In the autumn, when the breeding season is over, you can often see house martins perching on wires.

These house martins are preparing for their long journey back to Africa. You can tell them apart from swallows by their short forked tails and white chins.

Woodpeckers

If you live near an area where there are some large trees, listen out for the sound of drumming in the distance. You can often hear woodpeckers before you see them!

Great spots

The great spotted woodpecker is the most common woodpecker in Britain. It's also the loudest drummer! Look out for a flash of black, white and red as it flies from tree to tree.

Drumming and drilling

Most male birds use their voices to claim their territory and attract a mate, but woodpeckers use their beaks. They bash them against hollow trees and dead wood to make loud drumming sounds. They also use their beaks to drill nest holes in trees and find insect grubs and beetles to eat.

Drumming time

Great spotted woodpeckers may drum as many as 600 times a day. The best time to hear them is in the spring.

If you get close to a great spotted woodpecker, you will see its smart black-and-white plumage and the red patch below its tail.

Cuckoos

As soon as you hear the sound of a cuckoo – 'cuc-koo, cuc-koo' – you know spring has arrived. Everyone loves its cheery call, but did you know the cuckoo has a cunning side?

Crafty cuckoos

Many birds spend weeks building their nests and feeding their young. Not the cuckoo! Cuckoos have a cunning way of making other birds do the parenting for them.

Egg deception

A female cuckoo lays her eggs in the nests of other birds. First, she removes one of the eggs that is already in the nest, and then lays one of her own in its place. She leaves her egg to be looked after by the other birds, who have no idea what she has done!

Can you spot the cuckoo's egg in this nest? Cuckoos can make their eggs look similar to the other eggs in the nest.

Seasonal sound

Listen for the first cuckoos calling in April and early May. This is when they arrive in Britain, after spending the winter in Africa.

The cuckoo is about the size of a dove.

Pigeons and doves

Wherever you live in Britain, you're sure to have pigeons as neighbours. It's easy to take them for granted, but these are surprisingly interesting birds, with strikingly beautiful plumage.

Urban pigeons

The most familiar pigeons in Britain are probably the **feral** pigeons that we see in our towns and cities. Of all British birds, the feral pigeon is the most **urban**. You can find them on streets, in city squares and even in underground railway stations.

Pigeon plumage

Next time you see a group of feral pigeons, have a close look at their feathers. You will notice a great variety of patterns and colours.

Homing pigeons

The first feral pigeons were escapees from groups of **domesticated** rock doves. Rock doves have a special ability to find their way home over long distances. They have been kept by humans for thousands of years and used for racing and to carry messages in wars.

A feral pigeon's neck feathers often have a beautiful green and purple sheen.

You can recognise a wood pigeon by the white patch on the side of its neck.

Garden guests

You'll know a wood pigeon is nearby if you hear its five-note 'coo-COO-coo, coo-coo' call. These large pigeons have become regular visitors to gardens in recent years. For some people they are unwelcome garden guests, as they gobble up large amounts of food left out for smaller birds.

Collared couple

Doves are in the same family of birds as pigeons. You have probably heard the repetitive, three-note 'cu-COO-cu' call of collared doves. Some people say it sounds like a bored football fan shouting 'u-NI-ted, u-NI-ted'.

You will often see collared doves (below) in pairs. They have pinky-grey feathers and a distinctive black 'collar' at the back of their necks.

19

The crow family

Your neighbourhood is sure to be home to some members of the crow family. They may not be the cutest or most popular British birds, but crows are the most intelligent.

Carrion crows

You are probably familiar with the all-black carrion crow. These birds live in almost every kind of habitat, from city centres to coasts. Listen for their grating 'kaa-kaa-kaa' calls.

Carrion crows eat just about anything they can find, from insects to dead animals, or carrion, and other birds' eggs.

Ragged rooks

Rooks are lively birds that nest in noisy **colonies** called rookeries. Look for their big, untidy nests in the treetops. If you see a rook up close, you might think it looks a bit scruffy. It has loose, ragged feathers at the top of its legs, which look a bit like baggy trousers. A carrion crow's feathers look a lot neater.

Like the carrion crow, the rook (above) is black, but its beak is paler, with a patch of bare skin at its base.

Brainy birds

Crows are among the most intelligent of all animals. They can use tools such as sticks to help them reach food, and some crows can even make hooks using twigs or by bending pieces of wire.

With their striking black-and-white feathers and long tails, magpies are probably the easiest members of the crow family to recognise.

Mischievous magpies

You have probably seen magpies boldly swaggering about in parks and gardens. They are also famous for their fondness for bright, shiny objects, which they carry off to their nests. They have even been known to steal rings and other jewellery left on windowsills.

Colourful jays

With their blue, pink and white feathers, jays are the most colourful crows in Britain, but they often stay hidden among woodland trees. The best time to spot them is in the autumn, when they collect acorns to bury in the ground. They return to their food stores in winter, when other food is scarce.

A jay can collect as many as 2,000 acorns during the autumn.

Birds of prey

Birds of prey are the meat-eating hunters of the skies. They have powerful talons, hooked beaks and fantastic eyesight for spotting their prey. One of the best ways of identifying them is to look at the way they fly.

Look out for kestrels hovering next to grassy verges near to motorways.

Hovering kestrels
If you see a bird hovering in mid-air, it's probably a kestrel. It keeps its head completely still as it hovers, even in strong winds. With its eyes fixed, it can skilfully pinpoint voles and other small animals in the grass below.

Gliding kites
The magnificent red kite is one of the largest birds of prey in Britain. Its long, broad wings are perfect for gliding gracefully over woodlands and hillsides. It feeds mainly on small animals, such as mice, shrews and rabbits.

If you see a red kite flying low, look out for its forked tail, the bold, white patches on its wings and its rusty coloured feathers.

Speedy peregrines

Peregrines are among the fastest creatures on Earth. When diving down to kill their prey, they reach speeds of up to 320 kph.

Diving peregrines

With their incredible hunting skills, peregrines are perhaps the most exciting of all birds of prey to watch. They will zoom through the air, and then suddenly dive down, or 'stoop', at great speed to kill other birds in mid-air.

City dwellers

Peregrines live mostly on coastal cliffs, but you can also see them whizzing through the air in many British cities. They nest on tall buildings, such as cathedrals, churches and high-rise apartment blocks.

From their lofty perches, peregrines have a perfect view of their favourite prey – pigeons.

Soaring eagles

Golden eagles are a very rare sight in Britain. There are only around 440 pairs breeding in the wild. You are most likely to see them in remote, mountainous areas of northwest Scotland and northwest England. With a massive **wingspan** of up to 2.3 m, these magnificent birds can soar through the sky with supreme ease.

This golden eagle is swooping down to grab some prey in its deadly talons.

Owls

With their big faces, large eyes and hooked beaks, owls are among the most unmistakable and fascinating of all birds found in Britain. These skilled predators can be a challenge to spot, but you might hear their hoots and screeches at night.

Tawny owls

Tawny owls are the most common owls in Britain. They live in places where there are lots of large trees, including woods, city parks and gardens. Like most owls, tawny owls are only active at night. Once the Sun has set, they set off to search for food.

During the day, tawny owls roost in trees. Their brown bodies can be very hard to see!

To-wit, too-woo

The hooting call of a tawny owl is one of the most recognisable of all bird sounds. Listen for a sharp 'to-wit' and a 'too-woo'. If you hear both sounds together, it's probably a female and male calling to each other.

Barn owls usually hunt at night, but you might see one flying low over farmland before dark.

Barn owls

For many people, the barn owl is Britain's most beautiful owl. Barn owls do not hoot. Instead, you might hear their eerie shrieks, which give them their other name: the screech owl.

Sound sense

If you get a good view of a barn owl, one of the first things you'll notice is its white, heart-shaped face. This acts a bit like a satellite dish, directing sounds into the owl's feather-covered ears. Barn owls have such good hearing that they can pinpoint small animals on the ground by sound alone.

Short-eared owls

The short-eared owl gets its name from the tufts of feathers on the top of its head. These look a bit like ears, but its real ears are under the feathers on the side of its head. Short-eared owls are not common in Britain, but in winter you might see one hunting over rough ground near to the coast. In summer, you are more likely to see them on moors and mountains.

If you see a short-eared owl close up, you will notice its bright yellow eyes.

Silent flight

Barn owls have a special ability to fly silently, so they can hear sounds made by small animals on the ground. They can glide without needing to flap their wings as often as most birds. Their wing feathers also have soft, fringed edges, so air can flow through them without making any noise.

Freshwater birds

If you have a pond, river or lake in your neighbourhood, you are sure to have seen some ducks, geese or swans. The name given to these birds is waterfowl. Another bird you might see near fresh water is the kingfisher.

Honking geese

Geese are a common sight in Britain's parks, as well as on lakes and rivers. The geese you're most likely to see are Canada geese. Listen for their loud honking as they fly overhead.

Mallard ducks

Have you ever fed mallard ducks at your local pond? Like other waterfowl, they have webbed feet, which work well as paddles in the water.

Male or female?

It's easy to tell male and female mallards apart. The male has a glossy, dark green head and a bright yellow beak. Females are speckled brown, and they have orange-and-black beaks.

Canada geese have long, black necks and white 'chin straps'.

You can spot mallards wherever there is fresh water.

With a wingspan measuring up to 2.4 m, the mute swan is Britain's largest bird.

Magnificent swans

Swans are among the best loved of all our waterfowl. The kind you are most likely to see in Britain are mute swans. The adults are huge birds, with all-white feathers, very long necks and orange-and-black bills.

Dazzling kingfishers

If you are walking by a river or stream, keep your eyes peeled for flashes of bright blue and orange. Spotting a kingfisher is a real treat. If you are lucky, you might see one sitting on a perch as it watches for prey in the water.

Fishing skills

A kingfisher is an excellent hunter. When it spots a fish, it dives down from its perch to grab it in its beak.

With its shiny blue and orange feathers and its long, pointed beak, a kingfisher is unlike any other British bird.

Hissing swans

The word 'mute' means 'silent'. Mute swans are silent most of the time, but they do make some sounds, including hisses if you get too close!

Birds of the sea and shore

Whatever the time of year, the British coast is a fantastic place to see many different kinds of birds. You might spot seabirds nesting on cliff-tops and huge flocks of wading birds feeding on muddy shores.

Seaside gulls

If you want a close view of a large bird, there's no better place to go than the seaside! Herring gulls are a familiar sight on British coasts. You can also see them inland, in towns and cities a long way from the sea.

Fish and chips

Herring gulls will eat just about anything, from fish they catch from the sea to chips they find lying on the beach! Those that live inland can often be seen **scavenging** on rubbish dumps.

In spring, herring gulls make large nests on cliff-tops.

You'll know herring gulls by their loud, squealing calls, their yellow beaks and white-and-grey plumage.

Clowns on the cliffs

Puffins are one of the easiest of all birds to recognise. You might think they look a little comical, with their huge, colourful bills and bright orange feet. Puffins rarely come close to the shore during the winter. The best time to look for them is in the summer, when they raise their young on grassy cliffs on northern and western coasts of Britain.

A puffin can hold lots of fish in its beak to feed to its young pufflings.

Oystercatcher

In autumn and winter, huge flocks of wading birds feed on small animals that live in the sand and mud on Britain's shores. With their black-and-white plumage and carrot-like bills, oystercatchers are among the most striking you will see.

Naming error

You might think that oystercatchers like to eat oysters. In fact, they much prefer mussels.

Oystercatchers have long legs for walking through deep water and long bills for reaching food in the sand and mud.

Watching birds

You don't need expensive equipment to enjoy watching birds. You really only need your eyes and your ears! But here are a few tips and hints that might help you.

Handy items

A pair of binoculars will help you see birds in the distance, and it's useful to have a notebook and pen for making notes about the birds you see. You can use a **field guide** to help you identify birds and find out more about them.

Spotting tips

It's a good idea to wear dull-coloured clothes, as this will make it harder for birds to see you. When you are walking through woods, walk quietly and stop often. Look for birds on the ground and on the trunks of trees, in the branches and in the air.

Bird clues

You may not always spot many birds, but you can often find clues they leave behind. Some birds, such as owls, swallow their food whole and then cough up anything they cannot **digest** as a **pellet**. Owl pellets often contain fur, feathers and small pieces of bone.

Feather collection

In spring and summer, many birds moult, or replace their feathers. This is a good time to make a collection of different feathers you find lying on the ground.

If you pull an owl pellet apart, you might see bones from the animal the owl has eaten.

Handling pellets and feathers

Always wash your hands thoroughly straight after handling bird pellets or feathers.

Classification of birds

To understand plants and animals, scientists look at their similarities and differences and sort them into groups. This is called classification.

Grouping plants and animals

Plants are divided into flowering plants and non-flowering plants. Animals are divided into those with backbones (vertebrates) and those without backbones (minibeasts or invertebrates).

Grouping vertebrates

Vertebrates are divided into five main groups (called classes). These classes include birds.

Vertebrates

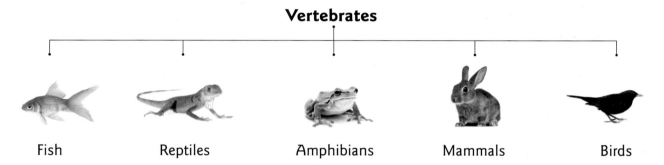

Fish   Reptiles   Amphibians   Mammals   Birds

From order to species

Birds with similar features are divided into around 28 smaller groups called orders (some of which are shown below). Over half of all birds belong to the order called perching birds, or passerines.

Birds

Perching birds   Waterfowl   Gulls   Doves and pigeons   Owls   Woodpeckers   Others

Orders are further divided into families. There are 82 families within the order of perching birds. Families are divided into genera. Species are the smallest groups – they are individual birds that are so similar that they can breed together. There are around 10,000 species of bird in the world.

Glossary

alarm call a warning sound made by a bird

breeding season the time of year when animals mate and produce young

colonies groups of birds or other animals that live together

digest to break down food in the body

domesticated of an animal that has been tamed and is used to living with people

eaves the overhanging edges of a roof

feral living in a wild state, especially after being domesticated

field guide a book used for identification

grubs the young of insects

habitat a place where animals or plants live

identify to discover what something is

lichen a simple plant that often grows on rocks, walls and trees

migrators birds that fly from one region to another in the summer and winter

moss a plant that has no flowers and grows in damp places

on the wing while flying

pellet a ball of undigested food that is produced by a bird of prey

predators animals that kill and eat other animals

prey an animal that is hunted by another animal for food

scavenging feeding on dead or decaying animals and waste

species a type of animal or plant that breeds with others of the same kind

spider silk a fine soft thread produced by spiders for making webs

talons strong claws

teasel a tall, prickly plant

territory land that is lived in by an animal

urban to do with a town or city

wading birds birds that live in watery habitats, often with long legs and long bills

wingspan the distance across a bird's wings

Index